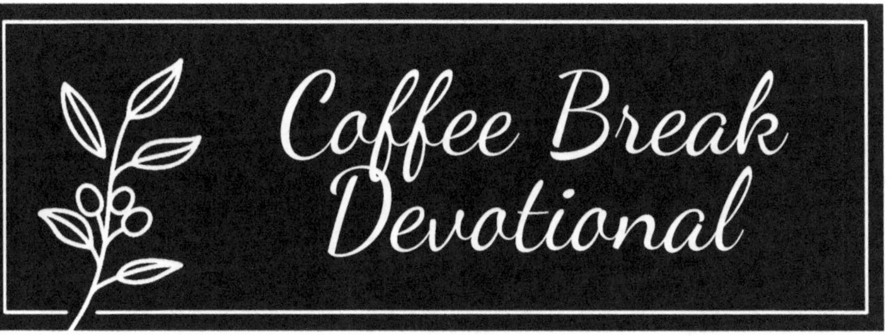

by Brenda Ford Biggs

Dorrance Publishing Co
585 Alpha Drive
Pittsburgh, PA 15238
Visit our website at www.dorrancebookstore.com

ISBN: 979-8-8881-2034-7
eISBN: 979-8-8881-2534-2

Art provided by Vecteezy.com

Contents

Devotional with Brenda Ford Biggs

Coffee Break is a little devotional before a meal to set your mood to begin saying grace.

Stop for a cup of coffee
With me today,
Before you begin to eat
And bow your head to pray.
It'll just take a minute
so take a seat,
Like an appetizer, taste
And see it's good.

First Week

God's Love

Romans 15:5 (NIV): "May the God who gives endurance and encouragement give you a spirit of love and peace."

I realize not everyone is emotionally strong. People addicted to drugs and alcohol are weakened by the desire for something that will remove the reality that life here on earth can be difficult. People can be cruel to one another. Families can be dysfunctional so we run to whatever will cover over our lack of love, friendship, and relationships.

Romans 15 tells us that we who are strong ought to bear with the failings of the weak and not to care only about ourselves. God gives us a spirit of love and His peace rests on us all. Love your neighbor as yourself.

Today may God's peace and love guide you to someone in need of your love and friendship.

God's Presence

II Corinthians 2:16, 17 (MSG): "We stand in God's presence when we speak. God looks us in the face."

Our conversation should be Christlike, but so many times when we are among close friends, we tend to lower our voices and gossip about someone we know outside of our clique. No matter how much you lower your voice, God hears every word. He's looking us in the face and shaking His head. We've let Him down. "Lord, forgive my tongue for speaking for Satan. Remove his control over my tongue and any other part of my body that dishonors your name. Make me aware of your presence around me."

Psalms 19:14: "May the words of my mouth and the meditations of my heart be pleasing in your sight, Oh Lord."

God's Faithfulness

Deuteronomy 31:6: "He will never leave you nor forsake you."

I am so thankful for all His promises, but this one is dear to my heart because I'm a widow with no children or family nearby. Sometimes loneliness creeps in when I feel isolated from another human being. One day in particular I was sitting in my chair looking at the backyard through the windows of my sunroom. The sun was shining, kissing the leaves of the trees with silver. Birds singing and flying from limb to limb, praising God for His faithfulness to them. Watching this scene, I wrote this poem.

> Jesus came by my place today.
> He said He was passing by and
> Heard that I was lonely
> So stopped by just to say, "Hi."
>
> He pointed out all the trees
> That grew in my backyard.
> All the beautiful flowers
> Bobbing their colorful heads.

I began to take notice
Of the beauty around my place.
To feel the gentle breeze as
It passed across my face.

I know now why Jesus
Came by my place today.
To show that His love
Surrounds me every day.

God's Joy

Psalms 65:8: "Where morning dawns and evenings fade, you call forth songs of joy."

From morning to evening I sing for joy of my salvation. The older I get, the less attractive the world becomes. The gravitational pull isn't as strong. A few years ago, I was flying on a plane to go visit my sister in Nebraska. It was a good day for flying till we hit turbulence that shook the plane like a roller-coaster ride, dropping several feet, then climbing up again. We finally cleared the turbulence and we were flying in friendly skies once more. I looked out the small window at the soft floating clouds and the checkerboard farmlands below and wondered if when we leave this earth, will it be like flying in a plane to new heights? I'm thankful that Jesus will lead me home. John 14:3.

God's Promise

I Peter 5:10: "After you have suffered a little while, God Himself will restore you and make you strong, firm and steadfast."

My husband was very sick for sixteen years, till the end of his life. He had throat cancer, which led to the removal of his larynx (voice box). He learned to speak by belching air from his stomach and formed words using his throat muscles. After years of struggling with that, he was diagnosed with Parkinson's disease. He finally had to go to a nursing home after fifteen years when I could no longer take care of him at home.

God's promises are meant to encourage us in our daily lives, and God keeps His promises. My husband has been gone six years, as well as my old familiar life as caregiver. This new life God has given me is the best years of my life. When Jesus turned water into wine at the wedding in Cana, the people said the groom saved the best wine for last. I am now strong, firm, and steadfast in my faith and my love for Jesus.

God's Creation

Psalms 100:3 (KJV): "Know ye that the Lord He is God. It is He who has made us, and not we ourselves; We are His people, and the sheep of His pasture."

It seems like all my life people have put me down. They said I was stupid and ignorant. I couldn't do anything right. I did my best but it never was good enough. I finally gave up trying to please others and thus began to believe what they said about me was right. 1 memorized this verse but didn't utilize the message. Later on in life I realized that God didn't make junk. We are made in His image and God is all-knowing. He is wisdom. I started telling myself this fact when I was 74 years old. I even had an IQ test to prove I wasn't what people said I was. I was who God said I was. I stepped out on faith and began to teach Bible study. I'm using the talents God gave me that were buried under the lies of jealousy. This devotional is the product of positive thinking. I believe in the God who created me. I am His workmanship. Psalms 139:13: "For He created my inmost being; .... I am fearfully and wonderfully made."

God's Sheep

Psalms 23:
1 "The Lord is my shepherd; I shall not want."
The Lord is my shepherd, that's all I want.

2 "He makes me to lie down in green pastures."
We do not voluntarily lie still—God has to make us.

"He leads me beside still waters."
He is my guide through difficult times, when nothing is moving forward.

3 "He restores my soul."
Our souls can be restored if we spend quiet time with Him, peacefully resting on the grassy riverbank, lying on our backs, arm under our heads, looking up at the sky with fluffy clouds floating by.

"He guides me in paths of righteousness for His name's sake."
God guides us through a purposeful life for His honor and glory.

4 "Even though I walk through the valley of the shadow of death…"

We walk through the valley of death, we don't die. We stay in its shadow, there's light nearby.

"I will fear no evil for thou art with me."
With Jesus by my side, whom shall I fear in Satan's domain?

"Your rod and your staff, they comfort me."
The rod of your discipline and staff of your Word comforts me.

5 "You prepare a table before me in the presence of my enemies."
You provide all my wants and desires while my enemies watch and wait for my ruin.

"You anoint my head with oil, my cup runneth over."
You pour out your blessings on my head and my heart overflows.

6 "Surely goodness and mercy shall follow me all the days of my life."
I will absolutely follow Jesus all my life, enjoying His goodness and mercy that is new every morning.

"And I will dwell in the house of the Lord forever."
Because of my faith in Christ's death on the cross, I will live with Him in heaven for all eternity. AMEN!

Second Week

God's Favor

Ecclesiastes 9:7: "Go, eat your food with gladness, and drink your wine with a joyful heart, for it is now that God favors what you do."

The last few years of my husband's life were very stressful. He had Parkinson's disease, among other things, which affected his mind. Nothing I did pleased him. I knew the disease was speaking—it wasn't really him. But I tried to do things his way in order to have peace. I would visit the nursing home every day and spend the day with him till bedtime. I felt defeated and I wasn't a good wife. I questioned my decision to put him in the nursing home. After he passed away I read this verse, which touched my heart and soul because God looked with favor on what I did and on what I do. His approval is what mattered to me.

God's Requirements

Micah 6:8: "And what does the Lord require of you? To act justly and to love mercy, and to walk humbly with your God."

A Christian friend was going through some difficult times and he asked me out of frustration, "What does God want from me? What does He want me to do?" Micah asked the same question, and the Bible says, "Act justly which means stop doing wrong. Be fair and truthful." Isaiah 1:16, 17 says: "Be kind, forgiving, helpful. Show compassion where severity is expected." Be humble means to be respectful, meek, and without pride. And believe in Jesus, the Son of God (John 6:28, 29).

God's Winner Circle

Ephesians 6:8: "Because you know that the Lord will reward everyone for whatever good he does."

For all we know about the next life, this much is certain. The day Christ comes will be a day of reward. Those who went unknown on earth will be known in heaven. Those who never heard the cheers of men will hear the cheers of angels. Those who missed the blessings of a father will hear the blessings of their heavenly Father. The small will be great. The forgotten will be remembered. The unnoticed will be crowned and the faithful will be honored.

The winner's circle isn't reserved for a handful of the elite, but for a heaven full of God's children who "will receive the crown of life that God has promised to those who love Him" (James 1:12).

God's Calm

Mark 6:47-51: "Take courage. It is I. Don't be afraid."

This verse comes from the story of the disciples sailing across the Sea of Galilee after Jesus fed the five thousand. Jesus stayed behind to pray but told His disciples to go to the other shore. The wind kicked up over the waters and the waves made it difficult to row, straining to make headway. It was 3 A.M. Jesus knew they were struggling at the oars, so leaving the shore He walked out on the top of the water toward the boat. Jesus was just going to walk on over to the other shore so as not to put more weight in the boat. Seeing someone passing by their boat in the dark, they were terrified, thinking a ghost was after them. Jesus shouted to them, "Take courage. It is I. Don't be afraid." He then climbed into the boat to calm them down.

So, remember, when you feel like you are drowning in your problems, your "Lifeguard" can walk on water.

God's Transformation

Romans 12:2: "Do not conform any longer to the pattern of this world, but be transformed by the renewing of your mind."

In Shakespeare's play "As You Like It," Shakespeare takes the audience on a journey of the complete lifecycle of a human being, played out in different acts. When my husband died, that was when the curtain fell on my Act I. After a brief intermission, the curtain rose on Act II. This act was a mystery, I know not what role I would play but God was the director and I was to follow His lead. He directs His love to me by day and at night His song is with me—a prayer to the God of my life (Psalms 42:8). This second act is like nothing I've known in the first act. It's a mystery to me how God has forgiven my sins and transformed me by renewing my mind (Romans 12:2). I no longer live to the pattern of the world in Act I. In my mind in the first act, I was only good as a caregiver and useless for anything else except mental and physical abuse. In the second act, God changed my mindset by making me a child of the King through His love on the cross. Thank you, Father.

God's Table

II Samuel 9:7: "...you will always eat at my table."

In this story King Saul and his son, Jonathan, were killed in battle with the Philistines and the beaten Israelite army fled. Most of Saul's family were hunted down and killed in a civil war between the house of David and the house of Saul. Jonathan had a son named Mephibosheth (Me-phib-o-sheth). King David began his reign in Hebron in 1011 B.C., which was just and right for all his people. One day the king asked, "Is there anyone still left of the house of Saul to whom I can show kindness for Jonathan's sake?" A servant told David that the only one left was Mephibosheth, crippled son of Jonathan, in the city of Lo Debar, a rundown city near Hebron. When Mephibosheth was five years old, a servant grabbed up the boy to flee from the enemy but she stumbled down the palace steps and broke both of Mephibosheth's legs, which were never set so he could never walk. King David summoned him to the palace. When David saw him, he bowed down to pay him honor. Then the king told him he would restore all the land that belonged to his grandfather, Saul, and he would always eat at the king's table.

This reminded me what God has done for us. We were all warring against God and as unbelievers we tried to do things our own way. Our good deeds were as filthy rags till one day God summoned us to come to Him. With our salvation He restored our soul and said we will always eat at His table, in heaven and on earth. That's why we bow our heads and give thanks to God for our food.

God's Word

Deuteronomy. 31:6; Psalms 118:24; Proverbs 3:13; Proverbs 3:5-6; Isaiah 43:18; Isaiah 51:15; Matthew. 6:31-34; 1 Peter. 5:8; Genesis. 2:21. 9-verse medley Old Testament to New Testament and back.

(Deuteronomy. 31:16) God promises never to leave us nor forsake us. (Psalms 118:24) Each day is the day the Lord has made and given to us for a reason. God is in control! (Proverbs 3:13) We can't change yesterday—we can only do what we have to do today. (Proverbs. 3:5, 6) God is not at a loss as to what to do. He knows even when we don't. We must trust Him to lead us. He provides for all our needs. He provides doctors for when we're sick. If we don't go, then it's our fault we remain sick. We were not put on this earth for selfish pleasures, to just satisfy our desires. We were put here to help each other and to love the Lord and lead others to Him. (Isaiah 43:18) God tells us to never look back but press forward. Forget what is behind us. (Isaiah 51:15) God says, "I control the waves in the ocean, and I control your circumstances by helping you through difficulties." (Matthew 6:31) We have no guarantees in life. No promise of tomorrow. The Lord could come any hour and any day. I only live today. Tomorrow—

if it comes—will become today. (1 Peter 5:8) Satan is at work at the same time so it depends on us who we listen to. (Genesis 2:21, 22) God created a perfect body—then Satan contaminated it with sin from Adam and Eve till now.

Third Week

God's Pentecost

Leviticus 23:16: "Count off 50 days up to the day after the 7th Sabbath, and then present an offering of new grain to the Lord."

Have you ever wondered about Pentecost and what it means? I sure have. But that's because I never studied it. For the Jews in the Old Testament, it was a required feast to remember the close of the grain harvest. It was considered a Sabbath. They brought bread to the Lord baked with yeast (picture of the Holy Spirit). During Passover (which comes first) the bread was without yeast. Pentecost was a time to also remember the needy. Later, in early Christian centuries, it was regarded as a remembrance of the giving of the law on Mt. Sinai. Then in the New Testament in Acts 2:1, after Christ's resurrection and ascension, 120 Christians were all together in one place at Pentecost (April 1). The individual believers were for the first time baptized with the Holy Spirit into a unified spiritual church, likened to the body of Christ as the Head. So now we have Pentecost recalling the giving of the law and in the New Testament as the giving of the Holy Spirit to believers in the church age. In this day and time we need to celebrate Pentecost to remember God has written His law on our hearts and minds through His Holy Spirit. Romans 2:15 says: "Gentiles who do not have the Jewish law, do by nature things required by the law, they are a law for themselves. They show that the requirements by the law are written on their hearts and their minds (conscience), by the Holy Spirit."

God's Justification

Romans 5:1-5: "Since we have been justified through faith."

Growing up I used to say I was saved "Just as I am" (Justified). Christ's resurrection was proof that our sins are forgiven. Paul gives us five results of our salvation. (1) We have peace with God through Christ. (2) Through Christ we gained access by faith into His grace. (3) We now can stand in His grace. (4) We can rejoice in our sufferings because we know suffering produces perseverance, character, and hope. (5) We have hope that does not disappoint us because God POURS OUT His love into our hearts by the Holy Spirit, to whom He has given us.

God's Angels

Ephesians 3:10: "His intent was that now, through the church, the manifold wisdom of God should be made known to the rulers and authorities in the heavenly realms."

I always thought it would be great to be an angel. They could fly around heaven all day playing harps and helping God do His thing. Wouldn't that be great? But then as I read Ephesians, I found they lack understanding of earth people. I have trouble with that myself. But they don't know how easy it is to sin with Satan around all the time. They don't realize the joy we feel as we accept salvation. This present age is a mystery to them. But God has decided to enlighten the angels and all who are in the heavenly realm to see how the mystery is being worked out in action. How the Gentiles are called out as a people for His name, a Bride for His Son. That's the mystery. So the angels are observing us here below to learn of God's wisdom as He works with the Gentiles to give His grace to us according to His eternal purposes. I can hardly imagine the angels watching us and learning what humans go through to reach heaven with them.

God's Power

Jeremiah 51:15: "He made the earth by His power; He founded the world by His wisdom and stretched out the heavens by His understanding."

Thunderstorms used to scare me with all the lightning flashes and roaring thunder. Now I usually sleep through all the racket. Jeremiah 51:16 lets me know I'm not in danger–it's just God proving His power and letting us know He is still in control of the universe as well as our lives. Verse 16 says: "When He thunders, the waters in the heavens roar; He makes clouds rise from the ends of the earth." No matter how far I go from home, I always see the clouds of His breath like on a cold winter's day. "He sends lightning with the rain and brings out the wind from His store-houses," verse 17 says. Compared to God, every man is senseless and without knowledge.

God's Prayer

Matthew. 6:9: "Our Father, who art in Heaven," etc.

Our Father, who art in heaven (Go directly to God.)

Hallowed by thy name. (Express your respect.)

Thy kingdom come (Request that Jesus comes quickly to set up His kingdom.)

Thy will be done on earth as it is in heaven. (Pray that the heavenly conditions will exist on earth in the millennium. It's too wicked now.)

Give us this day our daily bread (Bless our dependence on God for physical and spiritual needs like our daily bread.)

And forgive us our debts (Confess our sins specifically.)

As we forgive our debtors (Help us to forgive as you forgive us so we can have fellowship with God.)

And lead us not into temptation (Help us to avoid any wrong-doing by our own ability.)

But deliver us from evil. (We desperately desire the power of God to defeat Satan.)

For Thine is the kingdom and the power and the glory forever. (This doxology tells us that all our prayers have no other foundation than God alone.)

God's Yoke

Matthew 11:28-30: "Come to me, all you who are weary and burdened, and I will give you rest. Take my yoke upon you and learn from me, for I am gentle and humble in heart, and you will find rest for your souls. For my yoke is easy and my burden is light."

I love these three verses. I can just hear Jesus' loving, tender voice saying these words. Jesus is saying, "Believe in me, all who are struggling to make a living and burdened with the load of cares in this world." Some are going hungry and sick without money for doctors and medicine. Cares are written on each face. Jesus says, "I'll give you rest. I'll ease your mind." He refers to His yoke, which is a double yoke made for two oxen—not just one. He'll do most of the pulling while you learn how to work alongside Jesus. You have to submit yourself to His will as you pull together. You will learn that Jesus is gentle and humble as He teaches what you should know. You will learn to rest when the work is done instead of tossing and turning because of all your troubles. You'll find it's easier in tandem with God than by working alone. You will learn to move with Him and go where He goes. God's influence and salvation will make life lighter and joyful.

God's Blessings

Matthew 5:3-10: "Blessed are the poor in spirit, for theirs is the kingdom of heaven."

The Beatitudes are the traits for each Christian to be happy. Blessed are the spiritually poor in spirit who rely on God's salvation, for they are forgiven and theirs is the kingdom of heaven. Blessed are those who mourn from past hurts, grief for the world's condition, and regrets for sins, for they will be comforted when God wipes away all tears. Blessed are those who are meek and humble, for they will inherit the new earth. Blessed are those who hunger and thirst for God and His righteous, for they will be filled and satisfied. Blessed are the merciful, who are compassionate to others—not judgmental, for they will be shown mercy when judged. Blessed are the pure in heart, whose conscience is clear because they are saved by Christ's blood, for they will see God. Blessed are the peacemakers, who actively intervene to make peace instead of watching on the sidelines, for they will be called sons of God by receiving Jesus Christ as Savior. Blessed are those who are persecuted, jailed, and killed as martyrs because of righteousness, for theirs is the kingdom of heaven. A great reward awaits the prophets and companions in the Tribulation and O.T. spokesmen who stood true in spite of persecution. The Beatitudes present a portrait of the ideal citizen in Christ's kingdom.

35

Fourth Week

God's Newness

Isaiah 43:18-19: "Forget the former things; Do not dwell on the past. See, I am doing a new thing! Now it springs up; Do you not perceive it?"

I've been hearing a lot about bullying on the news lately. With technology flourishing, it's worse now than it used to be. When I was growing up, I was a victim of bullying. As far back as I can remember I was teased, mocked, and verbally and mentally abused. No one would take up for me. I had to take it and ignore it. Even when I grew up and worked in an office, coworkers were bullies. I was taught that when I went to work that I should work as for the Lord. Whatever my hands found to do—do it with all diligence. That was my work ethic. There are only two reasons people will bully you: Either you did something to them or they are jealous of you. In my case, people were jealous of my work ethic, for which I received several awards. They weren't willing to change their ethics but instead wanted me to change mine. In time, God has blessed me beyond measure as I continue to serve the Lord, forgetting the past and allowing God to do a new thing in me. I perceive His hand working in my life. Thank you, Father.

God's Guidance

Isaiah 42:16 (NIV): "I will lead the blind (spiritually) by ways they have not known, along unfamiliar paths I will guide them; I will turn the darkness into light before them and make the rough places smooth."

The Christian life can be difficult sometimes because of circumstances beyond our control, like unbelieving family, a spouse, friends, or maybe a medical diagnosis. Or people at work who do not understand the things of God. "We can be sure that if God sends us over rocky roads, He will provide us with sturdy shoes. He will never send us on any journey without equipping us well." I have never seen a Christian serving the Lord with no ability to do the given job.

God's Gift

John 3:36: "Whoever believes in the Son has eternal life."

I was reading my Bible the other morning when I ran across this verse. I've read it a thousand times but this time I noticed it said "has," not "will have" or "when I die," it said "has" as in now! I am now living in eternity on earth and then just by walking through a door, I continue my life in another city. I won't know death because Psalms 23 says death is a shadowy valley or a fog I pass through going to my new home in another city. I'm still the person I was when I first believed in Jesus Christ. He's walked with me all these years, getting to know me, waiting for me to use up my allotted number of days here in this short section of eternity and then, hand in hand with Jesus, pass into the next section of eternity, which is much longer and more beautiful. He's as familiar with me now as He was when He died on the cross for me, and when I arrive in heaven He'll see a familiar face—me.

God's Teaching

Job 12:7-11: "But ask the animals and they will teach you, or the birds of the air, and they will tell you."

I enjoy watching birds and animals in their own habitat. It's unbelievable how they worship and obey His commands. The animals do not intermarry with other species like a horse with a pig, pig with a goat, etc. Birds also do not mix with other types of birds, like blue jays with robins, woodpeckers, and wrens. They all stay with their own kind. Fish with fish, whales with whales. Also, all animals bow their heads before eating—as we should. If human beings took lessons from the animal kingdom, there would not be such evil in the world. Homosexuality, thievery, immorality, etc. God wanted us to have life lessons, so He created the birds of the air and the animals as teachers.

God's Plans

Jeremiah 29:11: "I know the plans I have for you."

Ephesians 1:10: "For we are God's workmanship, created in Christ Jesus to do good works which God prepared in advance for us to do."

When a person finally realizes that God created them for a specific job since the creation of time, they need to figure out what that might mean. Each morning is a brand-new day, like the first days of creation. We need to ask ourselves, before getting out of bed, "What does God have planned for me today?" Remember, you will not experience anything or meet anyone that God has not prepared you in advance for.

God's Pasture

Psalms 100:3: "Know that the Lord is God. It is He who has made us and not we ourselves. We are His people, the sheep of His pasture."

I guess most people wonder who God is. His name is misused every day and in every way, as a curse and as a blessing. People need to stop and think who He is before uttering His name. He is the Perfect Being in power, wisdom, and goodness; Creator and Ruler of the universe; He is eternal; the before and after, Alpha and Omega; sustainer of all things. Once this definition sinks in, how can anyone be so casual in the use of His name? Can sheep rebel against the shepherd? No! The sheep hear their shepherd's voice and come running. We are God's sheep in His pasture. If we hear His voice, we need to come running, too.

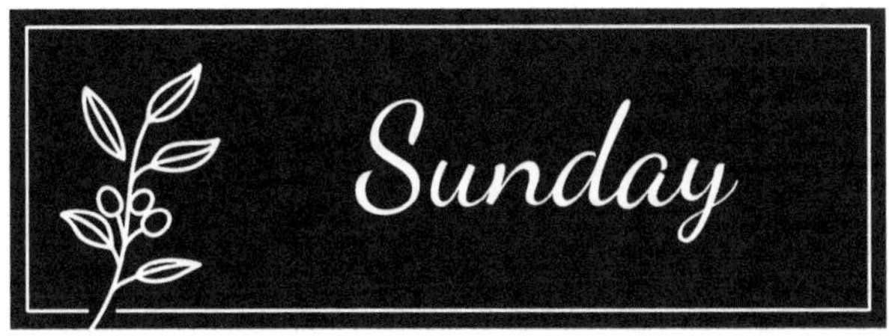

God's Bridge

Hebrews 10:24: "Let us consider how we may spur one another on toward love and good deeds ... but let us encourage one another—and all the more as you see the Day approaching."

I try to reach out to those people who are weakening in their faith because of the circumstances they find themselves in. Life can be a rough, winding road to travel. God's Word says we are to consider how we can help. We need to think carefully before making a decision on what to do so we don't make matters worse. We can share our stories with others to let them know they are not alone. The stories we share can build a relational bridge that Jesus can walk across from your heart to theirs. Then He is able to strengthen them and give them peace and comfort.

Fifth Week

God's Value

Psalms 139:16: "Your eyes saw my unformed body, all the days ordained for me were written in your book before one of them came to be."

According to this verse, God saw me as a tadpole in my mother's womb. Imagine that! I am so shy; I wouldn't think of anyone seeing me without makeup on or my hair combed and I'm dressed nicely. Yet God saw me as far back as to my first existence. He has all my days numbered and written in a divine book, everything I've ever said and done. He remembers when He came and saved me, too, regardless of how I looked. I am of value to Him because He sent His son to die for me and this "ugly duckling" gets to be where He is. Hallelujah! I pray He is pleased with what I've done with the days written in His book.

God's Search

Psalms 139:23: "Search me, O God, and know my heart; test me and know my anxious thoughts. See if there is any wicked way in me and lead me in the way everlasting."

It's hard for me to make decisions. I never know what the right thing to do should be. Is this God's will or my will? When it comes to spiritual decisions, I say this verse in prayer and song. Satan is always roaming around like a lion seeking whom he may devour, but the eyes of the Lord are also ranging throughout the earth to strengthen those whose hearts are fully committed to Him. II Chron. 16:9. God will win the search. Thank you, Father.

God's Thoughts

Psalms 139:17: "How precious to me are your thoughts, Oh God."

I can hardly imagine that God would take the time to think of me. I think of Him all the time because He is my Lord and Savior, but who am I? I'm the dust of the earth, and the Bible says, "How vast is the sum of His thoughts." He prays for me, too! Romans 8:32 says: "Christ Jesus who died and raised to life is at the right hand of God and is also interceding (praying) for us." I must keep Him busy with all His thoughts and prayers for me. I shall serve Him as best I can, as long as I can.

I hope you have enjoyed this small devotional along with your coffee. I would like to suggest that on the blank pages you can write notes, prayer requests, or your thoughts on the days reading. May God bless you as you read and draw closer to Him.

www.ingramcontent.com/pod-product-compliance
Lightning Source LLC
Chambersburg PA
CBHW051358150726
48000CB00003B/1241